PURSUIT
OF HONOR

PURSUIT
OF HONOR

Poems by
L. E. SISSMAN

An Atlantic Monthly Press Book
LITTLE, BROWN AND COMPANY · BOSTON · TORONTO

LIBRARY OF CONGRESS CATALOG CARD NO. 73-143709

T 04/71

FIRST EDITION

Of the poems in this collection, twelve appeared originally in *The New Yorker;* one in *Harper's;* four in the *Atlantic,* including the title poem.

ATLANTIC—LITTLE, BROWN BOOKS
ARE PUBLISHED BY
LITTLE, BROWN AND COMPANY
IN ASSOCIATION WITH
THE ATLANTIC MONTHLY PRESS

*Published simultaneously in Canada
by Little, Brown & Company (Canada) Limited*

PRINTED IN THE UNITED STATES OF AMERICA

For my mother and father

Contents

I

The Big Rock-Candy Mountain

(To the memory of my half brother, Winfield
Shannon, itinerant farm worker, 1909–69)

> A mason times his mallet
> to a lark's twitter . . .
> till the stone spells a name
> naming none,
> a man abolished.
>   — *Basil Bunting*

I.   "ON A SUMMER'S DAY IN THE MONTH OF MAY,
     A JOCKER COME A-HIKING
     DOWN A SHADY LANE IN THE SUGAR CANE,
     A-LOOKING FOR HIS LIKING. . . ."

The land was theirs after we were the land's,
The visionaries with prehensile hands —
The Wobblies, Okies, wetbacks — driven and drawn
To cross the land and see it, to select
A tree to lie out under: a Pound Sweet,
A Cox's Orange Pippin, a pecan,
Persimmon, Bartlett, quince, Bing, freestone, fig,
Grapefruit, Valencia. The trundling trains
That took their supercargo free are gone,
And so are they; a thousand circling camps
Down by the freight yards are dispersed, watchfires
Burnt out, inhabitants transshipped
To death or terminal respectability

In cold wards of the state, where their last rites
Are levied on the people, ritual
Gravediggers of the past, ratepayers for
A lot in potter's field. Old Gravensteins,
Bedight with morbid branches, shelter no
Transients at length. Our suburbs saw them go.

II.   "AS HE ROAMED ALONG, HE SANG A SONG
      OF THE LAND OF MILK AND HONEY,
      WHERE A BUM CAN STAY FOR MANY A DAY
      AND HE WON'T NEED ANY MONEY. . . ."

Uninterest in progress was their crime,
Short-circuited ambition. They came out
On a Traverse County hilltop one late-May
Morning and gave an involuntary shout
At those square miles of cherry blossom on
The slopes above the lake; exclaimed at wheat,
Fat in the ear and staggered in the wind,
In Hillsdale County; up in Washtenaw,
Spoke to the plough mules and the meadowlark
A little after dawn; in Lenawee,
Laughed at a foal's first grounding in the art
Of standing in the grass. Too tentative,
To deferent to put down roots beside
Us in our towns, outcast, outcaste, they rode
Out of our sight into the sheltering storm
Of their irrelevant reality:
Those leagues of fields out there beyond the pale
Fretting of cities, where, in prison clothes,
We cultivate our gardens for the rose
Of self redoubled, for the florid green
Of money succulent as cabbage leaves.
They have gone out to pasture. No one grieves.

III.   "OH, THE BUZZING OF THE BEES IN THE
          CIGARETTE TREES,
       THE SODA-WATER FOUNTAIN,
       THE LEMONADE SPRINGS WHERE THE BLUEBIRD
          SINGS
       IN THE BIG ROCK-CANDY MOUNTAIN . . ."

A young man on a Harley-Davidson
(An old one painted olive drab, with long-
Horn handlebars and a slab-sided tank),
You pushed your blond hair back one-handed when
You stopped and lit a Camel cigarette.
You laughed and showed white teeth; you had a blond
Mustache; wore cardigans and knickerbockers; wowed
The farm-town girls; drank beer; drew gracefully;
Fell, frothing at the mouth, in a grand mal
Seizure from time to time. In your small room
In Grandpa's house, you kept your goods: pastels,
A sketching block, a superheterodyne
Kit radio, a tin can full of parts,
A stack of *Popular Mechanics,* three
Kaywoodie pipes, an old Antonio
Y Cleopatra box for letters and
Receipts, a Rexall calendar with fat
Full moons controlling 1933.

IV.   "OH, THE FARMER AND HIS SON, THEY
          WERE ON THE RUN,
       TO THE HAYFIELD THEY WERE BOUNDING.
       SAID THE BUM TO THE SON, 'WHY DON'T
          YOU COME
       TO THAT BIG ROCK-CANDY MOUNTAIN?' . . ."

When Grandpa died and your employer died,
And the widow sold off his tax-loss horse farm
(Those Morgans being auctioned, going meek
To new grooms less deft-handed than you were,
To new frame stables and new riding rings),
You hit the road at fifty and alone
Struck out cross country lamely, too damned old
To keep up with the kids or keep out cold
Except with whiskey, cheap and strong. Too long
You hiked from job to picking job, and when
Snow plastered stubble laths, you holed up in
The Mapes Hotel for winter; did odd jobs
To keep in nips of Richmond Rye; dozed through
The night till spring; fared forward once again
To summer's manufactory, a mill
Of insect tickings on a field of gold,
And fall's great remnant store. Last winter, you
Spent your last winter in a coffining
Dead room on Third Street in Ann Arbor, where
Only the landlady climbed up your stair
And passed your unknocked door in sateen mules.

V. "SO THE VERY NEXT DAY THEY HIKED AWAY;
THE MILEPOSTS THEY KEPT COUNTING,
BUT THEY NEVER ARRIVED AT THE LEMONADE
TIDE
ON THE BIG ROCK-CANDY MOUNTAIN. . . ."

In Goebel's Funeral Home, where row on row
Of coffins lie at anchor, burning dark
Hulls — walnut, rosewood — on a light-blue tide
Of broadloom, we select Economy —
Gray fibreglass with a white-rayon shroud
And mainsheets — and stand out into the street,
Becalmed already in the April heat
That conjures greenness out of earthen fields,
Tips black twigs pink on trees, starts habit's sweat
Out of Midwestern brows. In Winfield's room,
A cave of unstirred air kept in the dark
By pinholed shades, we shift his transient
Things in a foredoomed hunt for permanent
Memorials. No photograph, no ring,
No watch, no diary, no effects. Nothing —
Beyond a mildewed pile of mackinaws
(On top) and boots (precipitated out) —
Except the lone cigar box. On its lid
A rampant Antony advances on
Bare-breasted Cleopatra, areoles
Red as lit panatelas, but inside,
Only a heap of fingered rent receipts,
On pale-green check stock, weights a linen pad
Of Woolworth letter paper. Here begins
Winfield's last letter, in a corn-grain-round,
School-Palmer-Method hand riven by age,

Drink, sickness: "April 17. Dear Folks —
The weather has warmed up some but I don't"
No more. The hospital bed intervened.
Peritonitis. Coma. Peaceful death.
In truth it is. In Goebel's viewing room
The guest has been laid out, now neat, now dressed —
In shirt, tie, jacket — as if for a feast.
It is not overstressed. He looks his age
(Not brotherly at all; avuncular,
Judicious, a thought sallow, robbed of the
Brilliance of his two straight and sky-blue eyes)
And takes his silent part upon the stage
Miming repose, an unemotional
Exit dictated by the prompter's page.
Later, in the three-car processional
To the old graveyard, we ride just behind
His Stygian Superior hearse, a Cadillac.
The grave has been dug under tamaracks;
The young Episcopalian minister
Dispassionately, as he should for one unknown
To him, says the set words designed to send
The dead off; soon the open grave will close,
The mason test his chisel and begin,
Tabula rasa, to cut that name in
To his blank slab of granite, much as that
Void grave will take the imprint of his weight,
And all his travels will be at an end.

ENVOY

But, prince that fortune turned into a toad,
Instead I see you — camped beside a road
Between old fruit trees in full bloom in May —

8

Lie out under an agèd Pound Sweet and
Sleep soundly on the last night of your way
Out of a rifled and abandoned land.

II

An E-Type on the Interstate

(For A. P. Klauer)

White needles wipe around their black-faced clock
Faces in unison. Ninety. The tach
Trembles on forty. Forty, I take stock
Of the houseful of time behind my back —
The scruffy luggage on the luggage rack,
Stuffed full of tears and sweatshirts, held by locks
Both temporal and spiritual, packed
To go to ground with — and am glad, ticktock,
To have outdistanced it. The road ahead
Is straight and empty, but a curled raccoon,
Unmarked, unmasked, caught in the wheels of noon,
Recalls tonight's appointment with the dead;
And I, rejoicing in the practiced aim
Of middle age, make haste toward the same.

Among Schoolchildren

. . . For Dockery a son, for me nothing,
Nothing with all a son's harsh patronage.
— *Philip Larkin*

I have no daughter. I desire none.
— *Weldon Kees*

I. ALTON B. PARKER SCHOOL: THE SENIOR MULTI-SERVICE CENTER

If forty is a perilous age, if it
Is knife and tightrope, watershed between
The steeps of early and late ages, it
Is still a coign of vantage, still a prime
Viewpoint to fall from. In the green-limed room
Under the Parker School, old people come
To get their lunch for fifty cents, the same
Hot sandwich, canned peas, milk, stale gingerbread
The children have just eaten. Suited in
Their bare respectability, they weave
With laden trays toward a greener room
Where chairs and tables are; are overhauled
By a long, giggling pigtail of small girls
En route to gym, who do not look at them
Or get looked back at. The old ones pursue
Their way to table, shed coats, sit and eat,
Secreting extra bread and milk in bags
For future reference. With honor and
The inner man both satisfied, they break
Sharply and jarringly with discipline,

And, to a piano deftly out of tune
And passably well-played by one of them,
Sing shamelessly old songs: "Smiles," "Over There,"
"Give My Regards to Broadway," "Tea for Two,"
And send one hour of a blue afternoon
To where all hours are, even those when tunes
Like those were new, and they were schoolchildren.

II.   WITH MASTERS AT THE RITZ

Punched in, puffed out, snowed on, embodied heads
From a class yearbook — shy of boyish lips
And shorn of down — bob shockingly up in
Rod Masters' narrow room and hand around
Their damp hands to be shaken, raise their damp,
Perspiring glasses high in tentative
Salutes to tenuous remembrances.
On a loud ground of voices, classmates change
Subjects and partners in a crabwise dance
In search of old acceptances, now void.
The women come in three kinds: stumpy, square
Careerist mothers lost in middle age
And not to be recalled as wives, beside
Their shining husbands most like firstborn sons;
The brittle girls of forty who fight rear-
Guard actions to retain each tooth and nail
Intact, and though succeeding in detail,
Immediately stake and lose it all
On one harsh giggle, a hysterical
Reaction to their striking torturer,
The steeple clock in Arlington Street Church;
The second wives, bland, smashing showpieces,

All under twenty-five, on whom it dawns
Now, if not earlier, that they will be
Conspicuously consumed by the proud, sad,
Bald men who ransomed them and their half-mad,
Half-envious coaevals. Masters takes
My elbow like my schoolfellow; his feat
Thumb-finger pressure thrills my funnybone.
His old child face, ascending like the moon
On these our revels, sunders in a grin
Of head-coach desperation at the load
Of youth we shoulder up the hill of old
Appearances — a smile of failing rage.

III.   A SEMINAR AT HILL

Tatnuck is set on seven hills, like Rome,
But differs otherwise. Its Capitoline,
For instance, is presided over by
A city hall in grafted Romanesque
Above the bare-bone granite skeletons
Of handsome, dead mill buildings whose last stand-
Still fell some forty years ago, above
Mechanic Street, where three-deckers surround
The small Hill campus, where old Tupper leads
Me out to meet inquisitors in beads,
Boots, beards, jeans, granny glasses. They sit in
Defensive order in four far-off rows;
I stand behind a holy podium
Above the groundlings and am introduced
And opened up to questions. None arrive.
No ex-cathedra judgments inspissate
The air from me to them. Impasse. I shunt
My stool out to the pit and sit in front

Of my non-interlocutors. Poor Tupper primes
The pump with his thin questions. Then one kid
Requires my views on Rod McKuen, which melt
Right in my mouth. I see Bob Dylan and
Paul Simon trembling on the tips of tongues
Like spring guns set to send me up. My own
Tongue's thick in transports of translation: strange
Terms — "like" as a conjunction, "bag," and "thing,"
In their nonce senses — seek to close the range
Between us, while a sobering sea change
Informs my questioners, appending "sir"
To phrases that increasingly grow square
As time wears on. Through no interpreter,
We speak each other's language to avoid
A confrontation, a concession, an
Exchange of terms across the bargaining
Table inside the truce tent. Met halfway,
And reassured our meeting is without
Result (that's how we said it would come out),
We go our several, vindicated ways.

Cock Robbins Opens in New York

Cock Robbins opens in New York: an amp
Big as the Empire State and a reverb
Vast as an echo up the Hudson make
Him and his downy nestlings known, if non-
Grata to citizens who swarm and hive
In marble halls beclouded by the fads
Of our days, stammered, tense, sensational,
Chameleonic, inescapable.
These ruffian boys late out of Eastcheap, in
Buffoonish finery, dundrearies, grins
That mock our laws of gravity, repeal
The compacts that compound our commonweal,
Try our rough justice and convict it of
Malfeasance, beat on every town-house door
In inquisition on our small hours, prove
Our age and majesty a legal fraud,
Pull down our high estate and kid our god,
Commence to play on the great stage of our
Most ornate music hall. The young arise
By rote with undiscriminating cries
To greet them; we retain our costly seats
And look on, exiled, as the music beats
Its way into our hearts, and the loud words
Reduce us to the pygmy status of
Outlanders in the land we sprang out of,
Unearthly excommunicants of love.

An American in Evans Country

(A garland of limp stamens for K.A. and R.C.)

Great men are big boys now; in retrograde
How sad steps they lead down the little girls
In fantasy to bed behind the shade

Of evening on the shingle, where the blade
Of night cuts off the vision of their pearls.
Great men are big boys now in retrograde:

Alone in regal rooms, beyond first aid,
They take their alter egos, lapt in curls,
In fantasy to bed behind the shade.

When dawn begins its daily, brazen raid,
Their godhead his pink forehead re-unfurls:
Great men are big boys now in retrograde.

Philanderers are reborn, but never made
By human hands, except the hand that hurls
A fantasy to bed behind the shade

Of age approaching, appetite turned jade,
Desire digested in the maelstrom's whorls.
Great men are big boys now in retrograde,
In fantasy, in bed behind the shade.

First N.Y. Showing

Think of those homosexuals at the Park-Bryant, think of them
At the All-Male Film Festival, Continuous 9:45 A.M.
To Midnite. Think of them in a transport of being received
By their kith, their kind, in being invited to
A show of their own, a show of their flag; of being deceived
By the tempter, the pander, the spectacled speculant who
Bids on, at lost-property auctions, the shape of their self —
Their only shape, really, preoccupation with self —
In brown-paper wrappings and ticketed, there on that shelf.

Manchester: Night

The cars spit past beside the Merrimack.
In Unk's Fine Foods & Liquors, a dim tank
Swimming with emptiness, strip-lit by night's
Dead shades, a dying waitress waits for me
In cancer's yellow livery. She stands
In silent service, messmates, till I call
For beer and Red-Hot Chile (sic). "A bowl!"
She cries across the waste of pastel booths,
And goes away as I plug in a dime
To play "Blue Tango" on the jukebox. Time
Resumes for three loud minutes and then stops.
Two women's voices fifty feet away
Trade August compliments like katydids,
Contesting who will pay. My supper comes
On wings of the stone angel from the hills —
The Uncanoonucs westward — where old graves
Still rear her likenesses incised in slate
Now losing its flyleaves. This stuff is hot,
As advertised. I sip my beer and eat,
Maintaining life in this void house of night,
Whose high green vault is battered by a moth.
Nine-thirty. My car must be ready now.
The waitress-mask takes shape beside me, worn
As currency, withdrawn, all but the form
Of flesh on bones, from life. Alas, farewell:

I leave a tip and pay the tart cashier
A dollar-sixty — chili and a beer —
And issue into Second Street, where cars
Full of the young idea ramp and roar
In social circulation on their strip,
Their clearing in the forest of the night
Made habitable by the humane light
Of Merit Gas, Zayre Stores, Ho-Jo's, and Unk's.

The New York Woman

The assistant editor of *Crewel World*
(The Needleworker's Helper, ABC
Paid circulation, 1-1-68,
1,007,773)
Heads home to lunch. In the diffusing lens
Of distance, her long face is pretty, young,
Unfingermarked; close up, it's pretty young,
But hatched with all the crosses of New York:
Divorce, childbearing, wishing, failing, work.
Beside her blue side, her small hand hangs on
To an enormous, tatty orange man's
Briefcase replete with fancyworkers' dreams:
Patterns, instructions, yarn lists, letters, schemes
Of art-struck readers to diffuse their cause
Across the country in a crewel crusade
To mend a ravelled world they never made.
Obliquely, Sarah stares into the dark
Inside her letter box and sees the light-
Er darkness of a letter. Hell, a bill.
Up marble treads she trudges, up until
A skylight drops a halo on her blond,
Untidy head. Palming a porcupine
Of bristling keys, she punctuates the stale
Air of the landing with a yielding Yale-
Lock cluck, and enters into 2½
Rms, rec redec, with fp, kit, and bth.

Her sad son's photo stares, reproaching her,
From grandma's farm above the gas-log fire;
The kitten, claws locked in an afghan, sleeps;
Her pink Picasso juggler mirrors her
Tight lines around the lips. She sighs and goes
To her Rollator-Top GE, which holds
Cat food, pork chops, a wizened chicken leg.
She eats the chicken cold and sips a cup
Of Instant Yuban. Hope, proceeding up
From her warm belly, lodges in her throat
And complicates her swallowing. She tries
A smile extravagantly on for size
And prudently foregoes it. The doorbell
We all sit tight for, powered by a dry cell,
Gives a cracked rattle, and she buzzes in
Her visitor, the editor of *Man,*
Not, as you might suppose, a sword in tan
And turtleneck, but quite instead a pale,
High-foreheaded, mild, intellectual-
Appearing, troubled mother's son named John.
And, judging from his step, he's drunk again.
He swoops in on the door — got it in one —
And espaliers her upon the whitewashed wall
In a facsimile of an embrace
Remembered from bad movies. Find her face,
John, and you'll be home free. Shook up, she smiles —
For real this time, like a Madonna does —
And softly scores him for his naughtiness.
He's all for bed; she's all for holding him
Off at arm's length, in her apartment's power,
And owning him with her eyes for an hour,
Until he charges out or falls asleep
On the rag rug beside the kitten's dish.
He falls asleep, as advertised by his
Stertorous radamacues. She gets her wish:

To skip her office afternoon and sit
In silence with another whose needs fit
Her pitiful and unsolicited
Gifts: doglike love, unlimited belief
In journeys' endings, tolerance for grief,
An aptitude for mothering, an art
As painstaking as any crewel heart.

Mouth-Organ Tunes:
The American Lost and Found

I. IN A HO-JO'S BY THE RIVER

This mouse-gray man with currant-black eyes stealing
Around the edges of his rimless glasses, stealing
Out of the restaurant behind his wife's gray raglan
Back and permanent-framed face — revealing
A world of middle tones suspent in mildness,
The lipless gray moue of the long-gone childless,
A rosebud button nose, the wild blue flaglets
Of March-air eyes impugned by reddish lashes,
The streambeds down each cheek in gouged meanders —
Now sidles past my elbow in lost motion,
All hesitant and tremblant, to the Flanders
Fields of parked cars to which a rootless nation
Repairs for movement and repose on Sundays.

II. AND DID THOSE FEET IN ANCIENT TIME WALK ON NEW ENGLAND'S MOUNTAINS GREEN?

Spring and an empty house and an empty spring-
House over the spring. A millstone for a door-
Step. Wind in slattern shutters. A thin green
Sheen in the dead grass ringlets, and a squill
Blowing beside the door, blue, blue. No paint since when.

The swayback barn — shed, really — open to
All comers. Hames inside. The pasture fence
Squandering stones on fields. The kitchen is
Savage: enamel coffeepot, a pile
Of yellow *Union-Leaders,* overalls
Stiff on a hook, cracked plates in the dry sink,
Bagged bluebottles in webs, an empty quart
Of Carling's and a Black Flag ant trap on
The pantry shelf. When purple lilacs last
In the dooryard bloomed, and Sirius early drooped
In the western sky in the night, Myles died.
This spring I mourn his unreturning pride.

III.   LIEDER EINES FAHRENDEN GESELLEN

Jesus, is Schimmer a flaky son of a bitch.
Listen what happened Friday. This is rich.
Friday he threw a party in his pent-
House. East End Avenue. Invitations went
Out one month early. All embossed, addressed
By secretaries, with — get this — a crest —
His monogram, for Christ's sake — on the flap.
Maida and I, we put on all this crap —
A costume party, *you* know. I was Gen-
Ghis Khan, she was the fair Maid Marian
In a green doublet slashed right down the front.
You should of seen it. Anyway, we went.
Got there right on the tick. Big hullaballoo
Already under way. Celebs. Champagne.
An eight-piece folk-rock combo. At least two
Bars in each room, pouring booze like rain.
And right in the sunken conversation pit
In the living room, there was this thing, floodlit

From up above: a funk-art statue of
A cop in a crash hat, standing above
A dead kid tangled in his motorbike,
All one side blood. I never seen the like,
It was so real. So still. It shook us up.
But we got over it and had a cup
Of Schimmer's punch and looked at his Jim Dines.
All of a sudden hell broke loose. At nine,
The dead-kid statue suddenly stood up,
Climbed on his bike and started it. The cop
Whipped out his gun and fired it as the kid
Took off out through the foyer. Panic! Did
That party ever come to a sudden stop!
Of course, it was a put-on. Schimmer hired
A couple actors. The bullets the cop fired
Were blanks. The blood was phony, too. What some
Wise bastards won't do just to have some fun.

IV.   GOOD INDIANS

When Radiation Therapy fills up
With gray lay figures, walking-stick insects
Pulsating feebly in the new blue chairs
And staring at the hangings, to the tune
Of gallows Muzak, then I know the big
Machine behind the lead doors, and the still
More powerful machine this whole thing is
Are working at capacity to take
The overflow from the end of the trail
And ferry it across the Little Big
Horn to the land of Nembutal, where sleep
Comes easy to such specimens as these.
Come, Mrs. Karsh, come, Mr. Bailet, let's

Put on our bathrobes and put down our bets
On a sure thing — the god in the machine —
Who will wish us away from this sad scene
And carry our spirits over the narrow seas.

The Dump: A Dream Come True

When Mrs. Finnan died, aged eighty-one,
In brave Brick Bottom, Somerville, her son
Did right by her: he called Kennealley in —
The funeral director — and had him
Take care of everything. (And so he did:
At the closed-coffin wake, he begged that Jim —
Who had his generation's taste — take just
One peek at her, to show Kennealley gave
Full value, even with a dear one whose
Face never would be seen. Jim did; a whore's
Pink-painted cheek shone out at him; "There!" said
Kennealley. "Wha'd I tell you? Hundred per cent.")
After the wake, Jim cleaned out her junk —
She was a pack rat — and took it to the dump
In his Ford wagon, cluttered to the eaves
With the sort of truck no one who ever grieves
Wants to hang on to: corsets, letters, lamps,
Black hats, bent saucepans, pie tins, cancelled stamps
From Eire, medicines, a heating pad.
At the town dump in Milton, Jim drove in
Through skeins of smoke and stopped beneath the rim
Of a semicircle of junkhills, on whose
Heights men emerged and, high and giant, strode
Down them to meet him. Close to, they were not
So formidable: half a dozen drunks,
Or winos, rather, each with his day's beard,
Each keeping back respectfully as Jim
Unlocked the tailgate and unloosed on them

His mother's treasure. As he worked, one man
Touched his brown cap and asked, "Is it a death?"
"Yes," Jim said. "It's a death." "A death. A death,"
The men around him echoed, and a grave
Smile lit their faces at a picker's dream.
Still they stood still. Jim emptied out the last
String-tied suitcases, souvenirs of Rye
Beach, bottles of elixir, Spanish combs.
He shut the tailgate. As he drove away,
His rear-view mirror showed him how the men,
No longer decent, static, claimed the piles
Of pickings for their own; how fortune smiles
On someone as the obverse of her frown.

III

Tears at Korvette's

Inevitably, in Fifth Avenue
The past comes up to strike me like a rake
Stepped on in innocence: before my eyes,
Stung by the brusque repeal of fifteen years,
My old friend-enemy Gerson appears
To me in perigee, orbiting near
My earth for the first time in many moons
At undiminished speed, looking the same
At forty as at twenty, full of blame
And waste and numinosity and flame.
But now, he indicates, the tide is caught
At full and harnessed to his errant art,
Filling, last summer, a bare gallery
In Boothbay with a lone epiphany,
A one-man manifestation, a late show.
Soon, maybe, Hirschl, Adler, Perls will cast
Their tender shadows in his way at last —
"But come on in with me. I got to shop
For toys. My daughter's birthday." In Korvette's,
Talking impasto and Cezanne and reds,
Wearing a single paint spot of gamboge
For buttonhole on his blue blazer, badge
Of art in action, Gerson picks his toys —
Plush Mr. Rabbit (up to seven years),
A Dolly Tea Set and Miss Tiny Tears —
And pays with big bills scattered from his hand,
And leaves with bundles cumbering each arm,
And says good-bye with a sad flash of charm,
And leaves, a divorcé, for his hotel
And Nancy's birthday party, held among
Those canvases which were not for so long.

The Time in Venezuela

Caracas roads: the wind blows out to sea,
Reminding us that cross roads really cross
And go their ways unsensible of loss,
Just as, one numbered day, you must cross me.

And then I must stand out to sea and turn
Which way wind favors into other ports.
Enormous item in the heart's thick torts:
The dead-slow passage out of haven, when we learn.

Learn the crook backs of dock cranes, mile on mile;
The bitter pills of storage tanks; the fat
Flames of waste gases; the grand, greasy *jatte*
Of Venezuela. And unlearn your smile.

Letter from Coast to Coast

Alone and lately loitering beside
The margin of our Old Swan Swamp, between
Cattails' exclams and periodic green
Sleeves of slack water dotted with wood duck,
I hear a joyous and archaic noise
As you plane down and drop your PBY,
Still rocking, at my feet, and clamber out,
Still twenty-four, in ensign's whites and white
Limp cap bereft of wire, to share your pint
(Green River) with me. Since it is not so,
It never happened, and instead you go,
At forty-three, a lost alumnus, to
The wildwood of Los Angeles to take
A new, maybe a false, identity,
Why then I'll reconstrue you from the start
In hopes of finding you yourself again.
Scene One: interior: a vaulted, bare
Chicago armory; in middle air,
The film-winged monoplane which you have built
Outflies all opposition, hangs aloft
Far longer than the others, and you win.
Scene Two: exterior: night: playing fields
At an Ohio college, '39.
You, freshman rebel against discipline's
Old sanctions, scourge of upperclassmen, rash
Defender of the innocents, are pursued
By armies of your enemies as you run,

Buck-naked, through the end zone and across
Dim yard lines up the field. (You said you thought
That you were flying then; but you were caught
And, laughing, dunked in gallons of deck paint
To make a coat of many colors.) Three:
Interior: Iowa City: Primary
School husbands yellow Stearmans in the ag-
Ricultural college of the corn for miles
Around, around the Hawkeye Hotel room
Where you, on liberty, set up your house
Of love, your folding, falling portable
Cardhouse, your desert tent, your home, with a
Slight girl who knew the words straight off the farm
(A waitress at the Maquoketa Grille),
Whose mouth spoke all unmade-up words, whose warm
Recipience built a mansion house among
The suffering furnishings, a house raised up
On Friday night, pulled down by Monday noon,
Where you would not in lordship walk again.
Four: Whidbey Island. Unforetold cascades
Of fog shield real Cascades, a point of not
Just passing interest to the flying boat
Between the sun, a soft-edged sovereign,
And the hard water, aqua regia,
Which solves all foreign bodiments which fall
Into its see, its jurisdiction. Full
Speed ahead, you climb to overtop
Putative mountains, sketch a new approach
Miles westward of the unseen beach, and turn
Into the wind, into a drunken dream
Of flight you wake from in Scene Five, upon
A couch in the Corpus Christi Officers' Club,
Where a mad captain damns your disarray,
Disgracing your gilt stripe, gilt star, gilt arm
Of service, and your gilded, grounded wings.

War's message ends; over and out, you ride
A Harley's pillion seat down dawn's Midway
Behind a fellow section man, who, rapt
In rye, noise, and discovery of hap,
Yells, "Even the weathervanes are pointing at
Us!" Seven: exterior, years after. New
England engrails in green the blue car you
Drive, laying down a screen of oil smoke,
On your appointive rounds as leader of
Bookish discussions led for learning's love
(And earning's gold, exiguously prized
Out of the firm foundation's flinty side
To keep your children in some penury).
Those children — Eight: interior — a scene
In your old house in Boston; your wife sits
In a chair out at elbows while she knits
Over her belly for the occupant,
And you withdraw to paper and descant
A poem on her state, about to bear,
Open and secret, far away and there.
Again — in our hotchpotic office, shared
In irony and raddled by disdain —
I see you lay aside your work and write
In verse, in longhand, on your own; your right
And dutied (ah, too heavily) mystery,
Too seldom exercised. Your history
Could end here, fashionably out of date
And indeterminate, but a new start,
A radical resection of your life —
New scene (Ten), new career, a brand-new wife —
Here supervenes. In California —
Imaginary only to my mind,
Untutored in fortissimos — I find
You new anew, a new-flown graduate

Embarking on your grand emprise. You write
Of life in space, in aerospace, beyond
Brakes, sprags, and clutches of our antique, fond
Twenties and thirties. I cannot pursue
Mastery that way; between me and you
The gap, once only continental, grows
Spatial and universal; in the prose
Of your curt letters I read new-wave verse
In a galactic Morse I cannot break.
I must retreat (cf. Scene One) and take
You as I found you, or I thought I did;
In the Still River swamp, my motives hid
By noble nature, I await the plane
Which, nonexistent, will not ever come.

SCENE TWELVE: INTERIOR: ENVOY

Prince of infortune, you come back to me
On our green terms by a black happenstance.
The phone rings in my study Sunday night.
It's you, clear clear across a continent
And crying. Your most sympathetic son —
Already paying on the note of his
Grave promise at sixteen — drove north last night
With a school buddy to inaugurate
The fishing season in the high rivers
With a first cast for trout; the singing line,
The Silver Doctor riding, diving under
The downbound water, registering a strike.
No plane came. Earlier, their station wagon —
Shooting the lacets of a Sierra highway —
Devolved upon an intermountain truck
U-turning, straddling the whole road, and struck
It broadside. Both were killed. Now, with your former

Wife, you maintain a mortifying vigil
Over the past and all its presents. Move
As you will in time and station, chance above
All designates your place. I sign this love.

New Year's, 1948

(Boston: Washington and Dover Streets)

ELEVEN

"I'm looking over a four-leaf clover
That I overlooked before," reiterates
The jukebox in the bar downstairs, which baits
Ladies with "Ladies Invited," but attracts
Thin seers nighted by their cataracts,
Snow-shovellers between white-collar jobs,
Purple-nosed punchers with ring-bounded brains,
And connoisseurs of California wines.
Up here we hear each clover leaflet fall
Between bouts with the El, whose braking wheels
Loose bob and treble bob and grandsire peals
In honor of the infant year, which springs
Out of this artless gallery of things
That we walk in, inspect, join, grasp, and leave,
Like the old year, with mourning on our sleeve.

TWELVE

For auld lang syne we take a tot of rum
And drain it toasting our hosts, Blanche and Slim,
And all our progeny, the days ahead,
Which, born in ice, swell into summer's bed
And dwindle into fall and ice again.
We toast discontinuity of pain;
The likelihood of trials recessed; the sense
Of living lightly in the present tense;

The touch of girls; the trenchant teeth of pens
Set loose on paper; the steep sum of men's
Expectance. With one toy hand, tiny Slim
Encinctures Blanche's high, wide, handsome bum;
With the unknowing other, he unveils
Arcana of the axillary tail
Of his erst mistress, Ardra Pease, and calls
For one more bumper to salute the wails
For a year dead and from a one newborn,
Whose daybooks our rude doings will adorn.

ONE

Beneath the aiguillettes and *fourragères*
Of the tall, leaning, browning Christmas tree
Sits a skin-covered birthday gift for me:
Bright Sally Sayward, once and again to be,
Perhaps, my stringent bedfellow, but now,
In intermission, the beloved of
The base recorder-maker, Jason Love,
Who flirts across the fogbound room with Nan
Milton, the playwright and remittance man,
The double agent whose much misprized name —
Hernando, actually — brought him Fame
In drag on his arm at the Beaux Arts Ball.
A noise of voices through the thin-skinned wall
Reminds us that the Linds are also here:
The zeta-shaped Greek scholar in a vest,
His woolly wife who would have won the West
One-handed, and her feminine friend, Tink,
Who now grows tipsy on a tiny drink
Of Mr. Boston gin and speaks in low
New Orleans tones, though she was born in Stowe.

TWO

"Well, happy birthday," Sally Sayward says,
Enduing me invisibly with bays,
Each leaf to mark a year. "Now, go away,"
She tells me, twenty, but, near-man, I stay
To press my case with passive rhetoric
Where deeds are needed. Nonetheless, her quick
Rejection is retracted. By degrees,
I talk my way down to my bony knees
And kneel and squat and sit beside her, where
My drinkless hand can infiltrate her hair
And fathom her resistance. Soon her square
Mouth may traverse to meet my mouth, and then,
Our crossed stars nodding, we'll be off again.

THREE

Drink drives my doze as, bedded, I embrace
An overcoat called Sally, and awake
With a harsh cry of fraud. She's gone. I rise
And steer, dead-reckoned, by the beam of noise
That issues from next door. But she's not there —
In the loud night, out of my borrowed bed,
Sally, my quarry, with her Love has fled,
And left me odd among these couples who
Now settle down till morning in the blue
Shadows and crannies of each other, while
I hunt the yellow bathroom down the hall.
Wind shakes that jaundiced box like dice: the glass
Skylight screams, hums, and hisses in the first
Blast of the first squall of the baby year;
The bare bulb curvets on its furry chain;

Chill takes my ruddy knees; a dust sifts down,
Which turns out to be snow; I stand and head
Back to my horizontal cloakroom, bed.

FOUR

I'm taking Sally Sayward out to lunch.
Inside the Union — say, this place has changed
Since I last ate here; look at all those wild
Magenta murals on the walls — all eyes
Lock onto us, the hunter and his prey
Brought back alive, if only for a day,
A date, a lunch, a showing-up of all
The bucks and stags stuffed in that musty hall.
We march abreast, my hand dressed on her arm,
My eyes right on her onionskin disdain,
Toward the serving line, where old colleens
Stand and deliver soup, slaw, salad greens,
Lamb patties, peas, beets, coffee, brick ice cream.
This round room has changed, too; it's lavender,
Sashed with long draperies in jungle green.
Look — there's a blood-red change booth with a brass
Wicket enclosing money and a man.
We step up to get nickels. The change man
Becomes my father. Recognition. Up
Goes the gold wicket, bang!, and out he shouts —
Face lit with flame, no doubt a trick of the
Sensational décor — "No, no, no, no!"
Dream ends. Escapement of small hours resumes.

FIVE

Doze, wake, and entertain those sawed-off dreams
That spring on you at morning, when all things
Distort and shiver; men on stilted legs
Mutate into short blobs, and blots explode
Into thin alphabets of wiry stars;
Simples turn double, petals form whole heads
Of leaves like cabbages, perspectives go
Back to beginnings like a Chirico,
And you fall down the fun-house chute of sleep,
And land, awake, in trouble, on the street
Of dreams, where every door turns you away
To face the undeclared but actual day.

SIX

To tiptoe through the tulip shapes of coats
Flung down upon and under snorters in
The clover-overlookers' den, the long
Coach corridor of their thin railroad flat,
Is difficult when hung, re-drunk on cold
Flat water, bearded, shod in dirty socks,
Laden with leaden shoes. I snap the locks
Back thunderously, fire myself out through
The door with a grand slam, and gravitate
Down to the vestibule to don my shoes.
The street is infinitely sinister:
A lamp ticks like a clock; the wind harps on
The stanchions of the El; a taxicab
Creeps, cruising, up on me; a sewer fumes.
I walk quite quick. In leeward doorways, eyes
Of derelicts move with me, and the lees
Of their bare bottles glint in ricochets

Of public power and light. At Berkeley Street,
Brick rooming houses stop. Ahead, the bulk
Of the John Hancock, lately dried and signed,
Inscribed across the top with Christmas lights,
Picks itself out in density against
The slightest lightening of sky. It's cold.
I trot, borne on a heavy wave of air,
Down St. James Street and into angular
Park Square, where, halfway home to Pinckney Street,
I stop for coffee at the Waldorf Lunch
And sit in solace with the morning bunch
Of regulars — red cop, green grandmother
With three bags full, brown lavatory boy,
White rummy with a tie, black counterman,
Pocked yellow cook presiding over fire —
All busy keeping an ice age away
From their cold hearts while waiting for the day
To break and bring in a gilt-edged new year.

Dying: A Resurrection, 1969

When ambient death came in out of the cold
And laid a glove on me in our rematch,
I covered in a trice the rest of the road
Before me, and at the end of the steel pier
I walked the final board feet of the plank,
Lapped in injustice like St. Elmo's fire.
Abridged, I burned with moral purpose, seethed
With fever to persist, sang angry songs
Of vengeful, mutinous futility,
Slowed my halt feet to a dead march, prolonged
The bittersweetness of each breath, paroled
Myself with garlands of last words. The day,
Freckled with birds in grasses, ripe with life,
Infinitesimal and infinite,
Hung on the hinge of me; the night, mooning
Over its lover, soon to be lost at sea,
Reproached me darkly in its waning hours.
When, purged of anything but regret, I fell
Into the ocean's arms, a curling swell
Swept me back safe ashore to wake ashamed
Of such dramatics, such forebodings, such
World-girdling ego. Sheepish revenant,
I crept back into life as into much
Too large a pair of trousers. Evident-
Ly even desperation leads a charmed
Life, valetudinarians go unharmed
At times, self-sorrow often sobs in vain,
And morrows rob us of our mortal pain.

IV

Pursuit of Honor, 1946

(To Anthony Hecht)

> The King of Hearts a broadsword bears,
>   The Queen of Hearts, a rose —
> Though why, not every gambler cares
>   Or cartomancer knows.
>
> Be beauty yours, be honour mine,
>   Yet sword and rose are one:
> Great emblems that in love combine
>   Until the dealing's done. . . .
> — *Robert Graves*

I. PROLEGOMENON

Fired out of Cambridge with a flat report
Above the cheering heads of friends, I fly —
Like any cannon-fathered aeronaut —
Out of the circus maximus where I
Made such a spectacle that I was shot
As an example. Figuratively, of course.
Now I skim south with sandbags of remorse

To ballast my high spirits as I hop
The hedges of Rowayton, Greenwich, Rye,
The merchant fleets of Westchester, the top
Of Bronx gasometers, and soon the high
Tors of Manhattan, which is where I stop.
Its streets spread hard arms into which I fall,
Another outlander who heard their call

Of anonymity and a new start
Among exponents of a single one
Pursued by corollary zeroes, part
Of everyman's megalopolitan
Birthright of passage. At the concrete heart
Of our discrete cosmogony, I light,
Fresh out of Eden on my maiden flight.

II. A TABLE DOWN AT CRONIN'S

In the beginning, at the Pentecost,
We five survivals sit down in the lost —
Whitsunday pinxit — distance where the crossed
Oars shine down on full fifty empty booths
Abandoned by their aestivating youths,
Except for us, Art, Nathan, Joe, Lou, Perce,
Their rearguard, now more than a drop the worse
For celibation and for acid ale.
Reading the *Summer News,* I blanch a pale
Fishbelly under my weak week-old beard
At seeing Honor's picture over *"Weird
Sisters* Shows a Profit," an account
Of the quite satisfactory amount
Her Radcliffe literary magazine
Rang up in blackmailed advertising. "Keen
On that one?" reading my struck look, divines
Sir Percival, my newfound British friend.
"Yeh, gone," interpolates sad Joe, my round,
Unworldly roommate. "Lessee that," says Nate,
Our blue-jawed, eremitic, Lincolnesque
Assyrian scholar. "That's a handsome head.
Where's she this summer?" "Home. New York."
    "Well, hell.

Why not go chase her? You can't let her cool
All summer. My advice is board your horse."
"You know, Lou," Art, our curate, our vicar-
Ious confessor ruminates, "he's right.
You should head down there posthaste and take up
Where you left off." "You'd all like that." "We
    would."
"Voyeurs!" "Uh-hunh. Just keep us posted." "What
A horny bunch by proxy." "Yes, indeed."
"Well, I give up. OK, I'll go. Who'll come
Along? You, Perce?" "Why not? I can't complete
My education till I've seen New York."
A feeling of well-being at a goal
In common, the electric brass-spice smell
Of a new round of brews, the sweat and *Nuit*
D'Amour of Mae, our waitress, the dimmed light
Of last-call warning, prologue to the night:
Thus the grand compact, sealed in Croft Cream Ale
At Whitsuntide, whereof I may not fail.

III.   EVENTS IN TRAIN

What is so rare as a journey in jejune
Anticipation of flat train fare, which
Teases the topless tower of ileum
With insubstantial visions of a rich,
Repletive borborygmogenesis?
None but a rough suspension of intent
Over the roadbed of the marshaling
Yard at the junction where beginnings shunt
And couple up to undistributed
Middles — mixed goods — bound for bad ends upon
Wrong roads. The waybill transitively joins

Our names up in its long petition for
A change of venue. In the hours of trial
Before our trials resume, Sir Percival
And I play gin, eat Butterfinger bars,
Read *Cue* for what's to come, and speculate,
Inside and out, en saga, on our great
Assault on the great world, which goes pitch dark,
Precociously, at 99th and Park.

IV.   ANSONIANA

A changing of the guard in Verdi Square:
Down, down through stratus strata of the air
Of evening, pink, hatched by flat plates of gray,
Sink, singing, emblems of an age that is
An Orphean underground now, in the dark
As to the names of archaeologers
Whose digs will bring it back to light in an
Age that awaits before. The armies of
The occupying hour patrol the shells
Of space and splendor, topped with turreted
Saltshakers, railed with Beardsley rays inked in
In Indian-ink lines, undried, aglint
With the sunk sun's farewell-performance tint
Of spark and ash. The beetling night watch heaves
Wide shoulders by, leading diminished legs
To timelier, if less immediate,
Haunts and resorts. The morbid discharge of
All arms of service, incongruent, skulks
Through unranked crowds of indeterminate
Station — brusque doubled-breasted men, isosceles
Girls tapering to ankles from the eaves
Of padded jackets, duodecimo

Editions known as children — to a strange
Place, home. My generation of the just-
Too-young to serve, the knowing connoisseurs
Of ration points, home-firers far behind
The unimagined fluid, bloody lines,
Are, on the other hand, at home at home
In six years' cumulus of dinginess,
Where best-dressed back and side go slightly thread-
Bare, paint peels down to primer, rust erupts
In small pocks on dim chrome. We take our way
West to the Hotel Henryk, a blasé
Trail through the shabby, civil wilderness
Of buildings whose great age has passed away.

V.   HONOR PERCEIVED

Pu we, to wit: a spring of throstle stops
Plashes unheard, implied, about the side-
Walk Café de la Paix, né Rumpelmayer's,
Beside the St. Moritz, a short trot from
The maidens' castle called the Barbizon,
Off-bounds to errant boys. The sun's sixth sense
Of increase on the first hot day of peace
Invests June's filles at tiny tables with
The mantle of mère earth, the mystery
Of all man manufacture. Sisterly
In their like cotton dirndls, poised to spring
Upon the season and to seize the day
And pick and press a leaf for memory,
They bat their fritillary eyes. A leap
Beneath my third shirt button indicates
That one of them is Honor. I present
My person, trussed in thongs of awkwardness,

To the blue justice of her unmoved eyes.
Her long mouth parts. A word falls out. A smile
Just liminally crosses the threshold
Of her thin lips and disappears. "Sit down."
I fold up like a shelter half. I'm in.

VI. 33 W. 58

In digs at dusk. A woman in the Wynd-
Ham semaphores toward us with a gin-
And-tonic in each hand. We sink back in-
To our apartment, much more populous
Than Perce and I account for: sumptuous
Brown bodies lean on walls, recline in chairs,
And even loiter on the pair of stairs
Up to the toilet. They are — just our luck —
Not jet nubilities, but instruments
Formed by a greater hand than ours to shape
Ephemeral, undying song: in short,
A grave consort of cellos and bass viols,
Left in our keeping by the sublessors
To shame and humble our indiscipline.
The radio's partita, filling in
Our chamber silence, coruscates with two
Spadassins' strokes, accelerando to
A bloody quick conclusion, and a mince
Voice comes on to report the upshot of
The first test at Bikini. A long boom
Takes several centuries to fill the room.

VII. DR. FISHER

Perce peels off east to pick up fair Elaine —
Dark Honor's late Miss Massey's Classes chum —
At a Park West address where mercury,
Hermetically limed in glass, burns night
Out on the heights of Siamese-twin towers
With bleak and minatory faces. I
Lope loosely northward on my two-gait feet,
A little overdue for Honor, through
Manhattan's second growth of tapestry-
Brick residence hotels and uniform
Apartment doormen fronting for the brass
Plates of professionals, the renting class
That God made doormen for, toward the door
(Brass, bet you anything, and manned) of her
Father's apartment house. That must be it:
The Corbin Arms, illuminated by
Three ravens statant noir upon a bend
Azure; in chief, a cor argent; below,
Natedna Realty Management. The boy
In his tight elevator and outsize
Cap braided "C" returns my skeptic look
And flies us slowly up to 12, where I'm
Expected or abandoned. The small brass
Knocker made like an anchor swings away
From my pursuing hand until I find
My fist just touching the low nose of an
Eccentric little man in evening dress —
White tie, top hat, and tails. The butler? "I —"
"You're Honor's friend. You're late." No
    servant, he.
"Come in, come in." So, Dr. Fisher, we
Are face to face at last. But not for long.

"Dear, I must run." Her dark face, conjured up
Out of a far room, makes a blandishing
Mock moue of disappointment. "Daddy, not
So soon. Why, Lou just got here." "Can't help that.
M-merlins won't forgive me if I'm late.
K-kiss." He scoops up Honor in one arm,
A Boston bag, apparently of tricks,
In his free hand, and kisses her upon
The parted lips, to my surprise. " 'Bye, love."
" 'Bye, Daddy. Hurry back." "Again," to me.
Door slams. "I'm sorry Daddy couldn't stay.
You'd love him. But tonight's his magic show."
"Magic?" "Yes. At the Merlin Society.
He's Warlock this year, so he does the show."
"He ever saw you in half?" "Lou, you're a pill.
Of course not. Daddy's eaten, but I saved
You some." Under a mounted swordfish once
Subdued by Dr. Fisher in Key West,
According to the plaque, I eat a steak
Now rather cool and well, while Honor serves
My needs with half a heart and sands my nerves
With sidelights on her old man and the sea.

VIII.   A GAME OF CARDS

The chair she sits in, like a Spanish throne —
A steal on sale at W. & J. Sloane —
Glows on the table, a waxed looking glass
Reflecting the divine diviner in
Reverse, muting her purple dress between
Two muted pillars of the alcove where
She now prepares to read my future. Her
Already dark hair shades to filaments

Of black laced with blue lights across the grain
Of the smug tabletop; behind her, there,
A tapestry of palms and pomegranates
Minutely wavers in the whistling air
Sent by a baby-blue electric fan
To promulgate her strong, invisible
Perfume among my senses and eclipse
The tune of flutes and obbligato oars:
The *Water Music* on the Vic. Oh, rare
For me, her Querent, that she now takes up
The pack and picks the King of Pentacles —
The glum professor with the money sign
Upon his orb — as my significator.
She shuffles, cuts three times, and lays the First
Card, muttering, "This covers him," upon
The King. It is the Queen of Wands, reversed:
An influence of opposition in
My inquiry. "This crosses him," she says,
Placing the Second Card across the First
To show my obstacles. It is the great
Magician, upside down, who threatens me
With a physician, madness, or disgrace.
"This crowns him." The High Priestess in her chair
Between two pillars represents the fair
One whom I sue for, object of my quest.
"This is beneath him." The Lovers, reversed,
Suggest foolish designs and failure as
The weak heart of the matter. The Fifth Card,
"This is behind him," is the Five of Swords,
A recent thrust against my fortune. Six —
"This is before him" — Knight of Pentacles,
Reversed, who signifies a brave man out
Of work. Touché. The Seventh Card. "Himself,"
Is me. Zero, The Fool, turns up, about
To step right off a cliff in his bêtise.

Eight is "His House," the tendencies at work
Upon the matter. Six of Pentacles:
The present can't be counted on. "His Hopes
And Fears" is Nine. The Four of Cups predicts
More contrarieties. At last the Tenth:
"What is to Come." Her facile hands turns up
The King of Cups, who warns me to beware
Of ill will from a man of standing, and
Hypocrisy disguised as help. The lock
Clicks back and Dr. Fisher lets himself
Back into his demesne. "But won't you stay
L-long enough to have a stirrup cup?"
"Sorry. Must run, sir." Peace. The charm's
    wound up.

IX. UP IN CENTRAL PARK

When Olmsted rested on the seventh day
And saw that it was good, he went away
To new commissions and abandoned his
Green Eden to such old pols as Parrott
(Who, in his civil goodness, framed and bought
Full many a journeyman in Albany)
And such new lovers as Perce and Elaine,
Soon to be scouted out of paradise
By a paterfamilial sergeant of police
To shelter in the cities of the plain
For having eaten of the knowing fruit,
The peach of each to each, which wasn't nice.
It wasn't quite like that, though, Perce reports
To me upon his prodigal return
At two or so a.m. "You can't conceive
How ludicrous it was. There lay Elaine,

Dying to shuffle off her moral coil,
And there stood I, embarrassed, pants in hand,
Couéing mightily to get a stand,
Suppressing laughter at the sight of her
Too bogus portrait of a succubus,
An *âme damnée*, poor strapping, pure Elaine.
I'd just commenced to button up my fly —
She was half-sitting with her dress awry
And looking furious, of course — when that
Great chuntering policeman shone his torch
Bang on my button-hand than then on her."
"You get run in?" "Arrested? No, just warned."
"It's over with Elaine, though?" "Not at all.
For some odd reason, my great chastity
Simply increased her ardor. We shall try
Conclusions again Sunday, she and I."

X.   E. 86

Kiss, kiss: a badminton of lips. We serve
Each other right on a banquette in back
Of the Carrara corridor of her
Aunt's old and elegant apartment house
Not too far from the Park. In the near-dark
Of one bronze flambeau flamed with a flame-shaped
Rose bulb of maybe twenty watts, we twine
Together, high on the new-pressed May wine
Of mouth and breath on ours, of breast to breast,
Soft license on inevitable bone.
Impromptu bowers are not secure; this one
Exposes us to elevator-waiters, all
The passengers in transit of the hall,
Alighters from, embarkers into cabs
And Cadillacs drawn up to and away

From the bronze doorway: *poules* with poodles on
Short leads, old, corporated Homburgers,
School-capped small boys with nurses, overdressed
Shoppers of fifty with antiqued, distressed
Visages under teased, tormented hair,
All seen in silhouette. The kissing stops:
The lack of setting for a second act
Halts our rehearsal on the verge of some
Unmanning pit of swelling, lickerish
Orchestral *tutti,* and sense brings us back,
Disheveled, breathless, to the leather bench
Where Honor murmured, *"Je vous aime,"* in
    French.

XI. LATE NEWS

Elaine, brought back by Perce as evidence
Of triumph just in time to interrupt
The midnight news with her own bulletins
Bespeaking siege and fall — what mangonels
Must have unhinged the wellsprings of her eyes
When Maybelline, once run, once smudged, now
    dries;
What catapults laid low those Parian
Pillars of Hercules, her two-stone thighs;
And what ballista cut the tethering string
That moored her tongue, which, linguimitted, flies —
And fills my ears with ancient histories
Of Honor and her father. "Don't you know
The story of his stammering?" "Well, no."
"Well, first of all, his wife was Vivien
Valenti, the Poughkeepsie poetess —"
"Um, 'What lads saddled me and rode away —' "

" 'In the odd hours I do not know.' Yeah. She
Married Roy Fisher when he was still a kid,
Just back from Old Vienna, starting out
As — what was it they called it — oh, an al-
Ienist. Seduced him, maybe. Anyway,
She died of languish or whatever all
Pale lady poets die of — drowned herself,
They say, in Lake Sebago — and left him
Alone with Honor. You can figure out
What happened after. Sure, Electra. First,
He had himself an ever-loving fling
With every lady patient he could join
On his official couch; but pretty soon
He realized there was no substitute
For his late wife. Except, of course, his own
Daughter, aged seventeen. That summer, we —
Honor and I and Maribel Cohane —
Went skinny-dipping mornings off the float
Back of the Fishers' camp. One morning, we
Felt we were being spied on. Sure enough,
The cattails parted, Dr. Fisher rose
To his full five-foot-two between them, and
Boomed out in his best voice (you know that cove
Can echo like a canyon), 'Honor, come
Back here this instant and put on your suit.
How dare you go in swimming in the muff?'
Those echoes. Silence. Laughter. I'm afraid
We tittered him back through the rushes. And
He's stammered ever since, at least with us."
The fisherman who lost his circumflex
And waded waist-deep in the stream of sex,
Casting his flies at any likely trout,
Was thus at last by his own line caught out.

XII. THE TOURNAMENT

Broadway, way in to too many tissue
Sections to count — the scruffy, canyonesque
Desertion of the fifties, the mock-swank
Ziggurats overlooking the poor mouse-
Brown brownstones tailing off down Fifty-ninth,
The crazed-white, glazed-brick, ex-Locomobile,
White, Marmon, Mercer, Pierce, Simplex
     showrooms
Divided by blank, mangy warehouses
(One sporting a half-scale Miss Liberty),
And the bombé facades of down-at-heel
Hotels still capped with clouds of verdigris —
Still boasts, a constant in all neighborhoods
And climes whatever, a bright, glorious bar,
Crawling with living colors, on each hand.
In each of these along the course of our
Up-Broadway walking tour to Honor's house,
Perce and I square off, face up, take a stand,
And down our ten-cent Rupperts, chug-a-lug.
Broadway, already skewed, comes more undone
And levitates at the periphery
Of vision as we doggedly slog on.
A draw: at Honor's street we calculate
Each has consumed an easy twenty-three
Glasses in transit. Oddly, Honor's not
That glad to see us; Dr. Fisher seems
Less cordial, if that's possible, than last
Time I came calling. Well, we know where we
Aren't wanted. Let us go then, you and me.

XIII. GONE AWAY

"Lou dear, I hate this place so much I can't
Describe it to you. Veddy-veddy beach
Club, strictly from 'So Little Time.' All my
Relations naturally belong — the ones
That Dad won't speak to. All the women (12
To 70) in unbecomingly
Brief bathing suits, and all the older men
In paunches and Coronas. They play gin
For high stakes steadily and keep one eye
Peeled for peeled ladies. All the younger ones —
My uncles, born with sterling-silver spoons —
Wear polo shirts with little college crests,
Play golf, and are weak characters. My aunts —
The worst of all — are beautifully groomed
And talk exclusively about 1) clothes,
2) other people's troubles, 3) their trials
With their domestics, *viz.,* 'They're always no-
Good anyway and think they're just as good
As anyone. Such children!' Speaking of
That — children — theirs, my cousins, are all dressed
And polished beautifully, not spoken to
Except commandingly, and *never* played
With. Lou, it's hell, and I'm so desperate
For the real world — or is it the other way
Around? — that I wish you'd sling me a rope
From that gaunt tower of yours. Nothing
    worthwhile
Till I come back to you. Miss me a lit-
Tle. Till New Hampshire, all my love, my own."

XIV. NORTH

A day coach made of barge boards, with a stove
Dead center. Musty plush. A clerestory
Of sooty lozenges, lunettes of blind-
Ing black. Moth-wing-white mantles of a Pintsch
Compressed-gas lighting system. Ricky-tick
Conductor jointed like a walking-stick
Insect, with silver glasses, silver punch,
And silver seat in his sere serge. A Pen-
Guin in my lap, I swot up Overshot
And Undershaft as the impoverished
Saltboxes tethered to the littered yards
Of marginal New Hampshire stage a fly-
Past and escape beyond the picture frame
Where Concord now spells out its static name.

XV. HONOR REPRIEVED

While Mim and Arthur, eager councillors,
Go at it hot and heavy in the Hawk
Hotel, or so we fantasize, we walk,
Moist hand in hand, up Main Street to the top
Of town, where we fall into a copse
Hard by the railroad tracks, and fall to fool-
Ing in the gloaming, testing Honor's rule.
Inviolable music of her spheres
Appearing serially — Saturn's moons —
Incites my astronomic eye, and I
Prepare to telescope myself into
Its promised land of origin, when O!
A bolt of cramp flung by retributive
Gods on Olympus or Chocorua
Hits me amidships, interdicts my fire,

And interjects me far into the mire
Of a green-rimmed dump-swamp, there to relieve
The thumbscrew pain. For Honor, a reprieve.

XVI. S.S. GASPÉ

"Lou, darling, it's more fun aboard the ship
Than I'd expected, though at night I miss
You more than I'd expected. Last night we —
Daddy and I — waltzed off, quite literal-
Ly, with the first prize at the Captain's dance:
A crude brass statuette of dancers on
A plastic plinth. Some handsome surgeon's son —
Columbia Presbyterian — 's making eyes
And overtures, but I've been cool. Miss me.
Must dash — late for the Captain's table. See
You in Cambridge, love, in twenty-three,
No, twenty-two days, or eternity."

XVII. LES ENFANTS DE THALIA

At summer's end, Colditz or Wintersborn
Flies its Oflag from icy battlements
Above the stifling balcony where Perce
And I, a farewell party, watch alone
And early one hot matin, the dead march
Of Rauffenstein, de Boeldieu, Maréchal,
And Rosenthal through black night and white day
In search of honor and/or freedom, pure
In word and deed as only the prewar
Was. They don't make them like that anymore.
Especially not Perce and I as we,
Shortened and shadowed by the midday sun,
Say terse adieux aboard Pier 83.

XVIII. HONOR PRESERVED

Light up the sky, Commander, where the west
Flares up, dies down, and deepens into one
Untinted, wind-bearing continuum;
Light up with the reflections of your red
Neonic name the shape of Honor's room;
And light the shape upon her single bed
Of our reunion. But the practiced key
Cannot, at last, unloose her private locks,
Unclasp her dots and hooks and eyes and stays,
Unveil her lunar marbles, lit by not
Blood from within, but neon from without.
No, no. "No, Lou, I've promised Daddy not
To do a thing both of us might regret.
I'm sorry, but it simply isn't right."
Right. Heart in hand, I nimbly say goodnight
And go out gently into that good night.

XIX. THE PASSING OF THE CUP

So, in the upshot, on St. Cyprian's
Feast day, hind-driven by the western wind,
I come to Cronin's, errant, seeking for
Old comrades, and find Joe already there,
Alone as I am, swigging Harvard Beer.
Some bragging on the summer's conquests; some
Shorthand dismissals of the girls of spring;
Silence and comfort, each of us knowing
The other has failed equally, New York
And Pittsburgh being equal in the eyes
Of the flint paymaster who doles girls' thighs
Out barely to the infantry of boys
Who mass about his wicket. We preserve

Our solidarity, virginity,
Hope dashed and risen, eagerness, and nerve.
Joe hands his mug fraternally to me.

XX.   LA TROMPE FINALE, 1969

Three-foot-high kings, queens, knaves with
    black-and-white
Photograph faces pasted in adorn
La Trompe's rude Breton walls: each king and
    queen
Of hearts is a romantic lead; each knave,
A juvenile. The diamonds are all
Industrial-financial types and wives;
The clubs are entertainers; and the spades
Are black celebrities. The maitre d'
Steers for my table, bringing, in his train,
Honor in Pucci, Guccis, and Sassoon
Hairdo, a little younger-looking than
I saw her last at twenty. " 'Lo, Lou." Face
Presented, seamless, for a glancing kiss;
Hair black and silver. Editor of *Grace,*
Glass of all fashion, arbitrix of form,
Tyrant whose imprimatur is the norm
For millions of fleeced sheep in their Dubuques,
Proposer and disposer of boutiques,
Hair men, hat men, shoe men, photographers,
Danseurs and dancers and biographers
Of taste, I bid you welcome to a taste
Of past en croûte: my ugly, aging face,
My parlor games with words, my petty pace —
An inch a day — toward obscurity.
Will that unman you? I'd not reckoned with
Your thoroughness, dear Honor. None could doubt

The realness of your interest, the thought
Behind your frown, the putting me at ease,
Except in context of the aim to please
And conquer. Ah, then, Honor, you have power —
The broadsword, not the red rose, in your bower —
But I hold honor, a weak, withered flower
In my pale, uncommanding, and free hand
As I ride out upon my bicycle,
In joker's silks, across the laughing land.

V

In Bardbury

(For John Malcolm Brinnin)

"This ere is what," says Mr. Carpenter,
The coffin foreman, in a herringbone
Waistcoat and gold-rimmed spectacles obtained
On the National Health, no doubt, "This ere is what —"
And points one digit to a neatly joined
And midget casket, just, to judge from the
Miasma of acetone, neatly cellulosed
In a suitable baby white, "This ere is what
We buried the remains of Mr. Eliot
In out there," pointing to the churchyard of
St. Muse. "And shockin little of im there was:
Two little volumes not ardly bigger than the
Basingstoke telephone book." With which he shook
His ploughshare nose and a colorless drop fell off.
"Now look at this ere:" a rod-long oak box,
Full fathom wide, wood dark as blackbeetles.
"This ere size is the one we ad to use
To plant the Poet Laureate, if you'll excuse
My French. More books than a ole libary."
Thanks, Mr. Carpenter, for the florin tour
Of Plume & Sons' back room. I point my broad-
Stub nose toward the moist, unpainted air
And pad out past the bone booths in their rows
To the green-grown, gray-pocked graveyard right out there,
Patrolled by stick-straight Mr. Sacrister
In his green-grown gray cerement.

"Two new memorials of special note
You'll wish to look at, sir," he says, by rote,
And courteously conducts my crofted arm
To one small marble marker, two by two,
Charged with her arms and "By Appointment to
H. M. the Queen her Poet Laureate."
The tumulus extends five yards in front of it.
A pause. Mist drips from lindens. My guide clears
His throat, discreet. "On this side, sir, we ave
The other monument." A minute's walk.
Above the tiny mound, a tall Trajan's
Column materializes out of moist
And pearl-gray air. A cool Ionic plinth
Incised with one chaste E. A fluted shaft
As great in girth as any tree, which shades
Up into thickening mist and disappears.
"Massive but tasteful, sir, I'd say." The yews
Drizzle in silence on St. Muse.

Convenient to Victoria

One night's stop at the Prince Consort Hotel
Is quite enough to entertain grim dreams
Long afterward of dissolute empires
Cracked, checked, and crazed amid the dusty plush
Of Ottomans in the tall drawing room;
Consumed in the ill-simulated flames
Of the electric fire; flushed down the puce
Throat of the toilet on the dais in
The vast and draughty ballroom-shaped bathroom;
Palpated, medicated, doctored, dead
In the sprung, ruptured king-and-queen-size bed.

An Arundel Footnote

(For P.L.)

"All that survives of us is love." Maybe
Not even that, it seems. Rising above
The glass case housing shilling relics of
This agèd and advanced church — art postcards,
Piper's pied altar duly reproduced,
Wide-eyed and side-whiskered accounts of how
The great spire toppled in a storm of wind —
There stands a rack of cheap guides. One depicts
The earl and countess supine on their tomb
And holding hands in perpetuity.
Alas, the facing text gives them away:
"Though many visitors to Chichester,"
It says, "are touched by this unique display
Of marital devotion, it is thought
That a Victorian mason rearranged
Their marble hands, once crossed upon each breast,
To meet and intertwine." Good night, sweet Fitz-
Alan, trapped in the prettifying power
Of a hypocoristic century
By its unloved assigns. All that survives
Of us and of our petrifying wives
For certain is a lying effigy.

A Life in Alabaster Street

His mad nurse pops pink bubble gum, and chews
On in deep beats — a metronome — to news
And rock on her transistor past all hours.
Far cars near, squealing, bent on merciless
Night errands, and redistance their dark powers
Up Brattle Street. Insane boys cackle by,
Incising their graffiti on the sky
In unknown tongues and accents. Wives next door
Beshrew lapsarian husbands, in the wrong
From the first fall of marriage. Down the long
Sword-arch of elms a party shatters out,
In tittering components, to the street.
Miles off, putrescent cities of the plain
Ignore the generous closing hours of pain
And violate the air with a cold green
Glow: worms and serpents. Dr. Wilmerdene
Moves, millimetrically, his light head
And faint eyes to the clock beside the bed
In his frame house in Alabaster Street,
Encouraged by false dawn. A.B., A.M.,
Ph.D., Litt.D. (hon., from U. of M. —
What a commencement *that* was), Wilmerdene
Decides to live till morning, meet one more
Sun in his father's window in his street
Besieged and stormed by madmen, who will not
Take him alive, however.
                          Phoebus, rise,
Precurred by sea-born Venus; regularize
A regulate life begun in unsurprise
And ended in confounding. But not quite:
Sun, dawn and touch his shutting eyes with light.

A Loss of Largess; Its Recapture
(And Point After)

(For John Updike)

Where are the belles of yestere'en, when Harkness
Reared Gothathletic pinnacles on darkness,
Where sate their dim dams in effasive, noctious
Harmonic bombazines, at least an octave
Over the battle? Where are those dames, dangled
On stringlings above mantels lit with bangled
Epergnes and lustres, ordering with mingled
Parade-ground basses and restraint-enstrangled
Triangle tingles of politesse their embalmy
Crack cakewalk waxwork corps d'élite of calmly
Extinguishing retainers going dark?
Today we have the proceeds in the park
Of their harbinging; in the standard carks
Conveyed by every face in every car
That laterals across from bar to bar,
Completed in the end zone of the high
Sixties; in the infirm plasticity
Of talltale fictions in the plastic city
Sent up, shot down (short life, short art) by those
Gallinulistic whooping cranes that raze
All parallelepipeds here below in G's
Good time, the sucaryllic by and by;

In how sad steps the dancers from the dance
At yon new discothèque take home, their pens-
Eroso tragic masks replaced to fie
Upon the desert teatray of the sky
And the uneasy vacuum of the street
Diminuendo to a dusty point
Of vanishing; in preternatural taints
Of outlandish unlikeness on each lass-
Itudinous pale pancake female face
Sub specie aeternitatis, less
Real than ideal in the race
For surety and demonstrata, damned
To disaffection and unravelling
In our unspacious, curt time-travelling.
Las! Las! Those belles wring out our witchèd larmes
Of lamentation for passé, accomp-
Li, done and done in in the niche of pomp
In progress ruckwards in the new-moon stone
Of night. Lick, lick, light, at the eastern hem
Of rich ink arrases, whose only son
Is born anew and dries our eyes with his
Frank, pink, unfaceable first sight; his light
Breeze dawns on us and islands us in calm,
Slow-moated selffulness. A fiddler crab
Crawls cancrizantally across the slab
Of pine to pencils, handsels one upright,
And imperceptively begins to write
On the blued goldfields of a legal pad —
Past Karnak, Babylon, Larissa, Rome,
Londinium, Firenze, Washington,
And the last sad daguerreotype of home
That the late holocaust consumed and curled —
The next line in the last act of the world.

Excuse for an Italian Sonnet

KLAIUS:
. . . I that was once the musique of these vallies,
So darkened am, that all my day is evening.
STREPHON:
. . . Me seemes I heare in these ill-changed forrests,
The nightingales doo learne of Owles their musique. . . .
— *Sidney*

This wretched mode, a huddle of untrue
Positions reminiscent of the way
Our generation stood, obscuring you,
Grown in the gathering evening of our day,
Who now rise to eclipse our withering view
Of perfect, present, future, and who may
Outlast us and accumulate our due
Deserts and honors, is a cell of clay
Confining us in our mortality,
A constant wailing wall to which we go
For counsel in insensibility,
A leaden treasury of what was so,
And may, in changefulness, no longer be:
A rectitudinal yes nearing no.

J. J.'s Levée, 1946

Awaking way up in the eaves of Lowell House,
Facing the East, where trouble always starts,
Opening his one blue eye to meet the sun's
One red one, J. J. crooks his back and farts.

His hand feels for the glass on the nightstand,
Ticking the empty glass of muscatel,
Finally finding the one with the blue glass
Eye rolling gently in the tiny swell.

Into its squirming socket with a suck
Just like a kiss his bogus eyeball goes;
Up he now sits and strips his T-shirt off
And picks black putty from between his toes.

Weighing one hundred ten pounds soaking wet
And standing five feet, seven inches tall,
With a pigeonhole in his chest big as your fist,
J. J. sings in his shower, "Bless 'em all."

He maps a life: first east from Central Square
(His point of origin), bachelor of arts
And master too, wit, rake, and bon viveur
And gift to every girl of foreign parts.

Then to get gray and great at the big feet
Of pundits, learning a hard new A, B, C
(The secret one that spells out man his fate),
In kindergarten to the Nth degree.

Now in his forty-dollar flannel suit
One size too big, and his one-dollar tie
One inch too wide, J. J. picks up his books
And goes right out to live and later die.

J. J.'S ENVOY

"All bleeding men and women ought to get
A bloody great gold medal for their pain
And duty in the face of certain death:
The Order of the W. C. with Chain."

In Baltimore—Why Baltimore?—
Did Kahn

A grisly torture dome decree, where Alf
Kahn made incisions in his secret self
Under the attic eaves. At work all day,
He'd bundle groceries down at the A
& P, hating such servitude; each night,
Up in his attic, by a ten-watt light,
He'd write, in anguish, ten more pained lines of
His monstrous opus "Succubus," his love,
His mother, wife, and children, youth, old age,
Past fury, present anger, permarage.
Stuprate, he rent his fabric with each kiss.
His pieces kissed again. No end to this.

Inflation

(For Alison Lurie)

I.

With a black manifesto of pistons, David became
Goliath: the small boy from English High
Grew giant and arched over neighborhoods
Of cheering followers, the president-
To-be of boroughs of new consciousness
Of his all-potent role. Time was when he
Licked fictions into shape at an unknown
Address, humbly petitioned publishers,
Modestly took his kudos when it came,
Tapped diffidently down the hall of fame
To meet his laurellers, and, amply crowned
And seated firstly on his dais, frowned.
But not for long: the conscience of a king
Is a quite different and distant thing
From that of an unknown; his majesty
Is self-propelling into grander spheres
That are undreamt-of in a commoner
Philosophy; the silver band of stars,
The brass choir of the sun, accompany
And herald his arrival at the throne,
Where a new paradigm of royalty
And secondary rights, created from
Unpromising materials — a coat
Upon a singing stick — holds sudden sway
Over the aerials of his old world.

II.

It is not easy, though, to wear that suit
Of lights, all heavy bullion and brocade,
Or to support that pointed two-edged sword
Stiff in its scabbard hard against one's side
Or to sustain the tiers of worshippers
Who people the arena with their cries.
One grows to fit the emperor's new clothes
In height, in girth, in lightning from the eyes;
Becomes a sort of grown-man's Santa Claus
For every season, flourishing his gifts
Eternally before the studio
Audience and his legion fans at home.

III.

Now no behavior is unknown to him:
On Cambridge Common, he exhorts the scum
Who turn a field of daisy faces up
To his rough sun and rain to follow him
To the moral ends of the earth in a dead march
Against our fathers' errors; later, comes
Home hung and splits his wife's lip with his fist
And drinks her blood in bed; at parties, cuts
Out wide-eyed girls from herds and topples them
On beds piled high with coats; runs, as a joke,
Or not a joke, for Congress, on a plank
Of endless drugs and love; records the moon
Shot as a phallic conquest of his own;
Transcends his old self at the Remington
Portable in his dirty furnished room
Not far from Fenway Park. From his town house

He looks down on the night lights of the land
He rose above, true to his promise, and,
Ah, like a comet through flame he moves entranced,
Wrapt in his music no bird song nor bough
Breaking with honey buds shall ever equal,
To us a legend, to himself a law.

VI

Empson Lieder

(For his sixty-fourth birthday)

I. LAW SONG

> Law makes long spokes of the short stakes of men.
> — "Legal Fiction"

We're all on different time scales. This clipboard
Will easily outlive me, given luck.
This house will, barring fire. The deep-set rock
Ledge that it rests on will no doubt endure
To the hundredth generation of our pure-
Eyed sons, if any. Only we are such
Short-timers, really, re-upped for a hitch
Indefinite in length, but not too long.
You will therefore please forgive my haunting song
Of awe at walking on the very bridge
Where Joe C., sporting his First Army badge,
Took taxi for the war in '44;
Of *frissons* at last sitting on the bench
Where Sally and I shared a Wursthaus lunch
Not too long after; of astonishment
At finding that the same key, pitted, bent,
Unlocks the same strongbox my father spent
The thirties filling with strange stamps; of love
At learning that the niches just above
The main floor of the library are still
Unstatued and available to fill
With our imaginings. Thereof my song,
Interior, quite tuneless, and unlong.

II. EVEN SONG

Not to have fire is to be a skin that shrills.
The complete fire is death. From partial fires
The waste remains, the waste remains and kills.
— "Missing Dates"

My unburnt hydrocarbons having made
A pall of killing smog, eftsoons I died
And came to Heaven. Sitting at the side
Of the great War Lord (a Brahms with sabre scars
Upon his temples and the porches of
His gun-deaf ears), I saw my residue
Coil mortally down there, a mustard gas,
Around the throats I'd failed to cut of those
Who'd cant incredibly through a half life,
Who'd twist on valiantly for penny gains,
Who'd trade you in on something more *courant,*
Who'd flee from those whom sometime they did seek,
Who'd go blind in the glitter of their rank
And brag that they had only them to thank
For such preferment, such an unctuous
Deathbed on shock absorbers, who'd find fault
With their subordinates for their results,
Who'd hang blame, like the shrike, upon a thorn,
Who'd lose touch with the urgencies of dawn,
Of leaf bud and leaf fall, of the small sun
Of February, the large moon of March,
The redwinged blackbird in the dying arch
Of elm, the great horned owl in the live pine.
A thunderstone, a bolt from the light black
Of my position high in Father's firm,
Struck them as lightning fingers of my late
Waste, left behind below. They died, of course.
Up here I heard the fat tires of the hearse
Fizz on the icy streets without remorse.

III. GIRL SONG

And now she cleans her teeth into the lake.
— "Camping Out"

Project her no projectile, plan nor man it.
— "To an Old Lady"

The heavenly body we once pointed for
In our near nonage — seen across a cyc
Of contrarieties in indigo,
An outer vast of obstacles whose fields
Of gravity press-ganged us into their
Cool marbles spinning in a gallery
And only barely let us go — is now
An older Merlin's lame familiar
Shorn of the charm of distance, bound to serve
Her homely, well-worn purpose, passion spent.
But yet, but now, a new low music moves
Her parts and person in a unison
Not heretofore perceived. "And now she cleans
Her teeth into the lake." That morning comes
When aching, groaning, feeling hateful from
Last night's exchanges, we turn angrily
Toward some matter-of-fact arising sound
She makes, and take a scourging wound, and see
In her shape, ground down by years of our eyes,
Our image twinned — the good we failed to do,
The bad we funked, the mediocrity
We killed our time on till it called a halt —
And love her for it, as we love ourselves.

IV. WAR SONG

This hint of anti-aircraft is disarmed
And as the fleets at a shot reascend
The eye orders their unreachable chaos
(The stars are moving like these duck, but slower,
Sublime, their tails absurd, their voices harsh). . . .
— "Flighting for Duck"

Great sheets of earth are inaccessible
To sounds of war; no man on earth is. I
Walk the back meadow where I used to walk
Before all this and find the fall leaves stilled,
The partridge drumming waning, the clear bray
Of crows diminuendo far away,
The very grasshoppers conservative
Of their small violins, the piano cows
Now lowing low, the dogs sparing of bays
And distant view hallos, and the rare men
Laconically calling in the fields
Seldom or never. But it is not they
Whose voices falter; it is I whose ears
Fill up, silt up, with war, and cannot hear
The nature of the world. At not quite dusk,
Our pond ducks — blacks and mallards — circle and
Splash down and leave me staring at the first
Stars, few, unconstellated, swaddled in
Buff smog, immobilized. Before the orange
Moon shoulders up gas strata, I can hear
One bullfrog pluck his bass string. In the void
Ensuing, single combat shakes the world.

V.   SWAN SONG

Then there is this civilising love of death . . .
—"Ignorance of Death"

The swan puts beauty in a picture frame
Of freshets, lilies, water-ratty banks,
Bullfrogs, bulrushes, and impending death
To hang upon the brain-gray walls of our
Study of consciousness. See how she glides
Down these far reaches of our state-approved,
Man-sanctioned nature, toteninsular;
How she gilds eddies by reflection; how
Her song is silent, pregnant in her throat;
How, under contract to our common-law
Employer, she must make at last her fare-
Well tour to pay the inland revenue
For all her rich, consuming idleness
Before our eyes, for all these books of hours
Burnt in the loyal service of her grace.
Then she will sing — Opus Posthumous — and
We'll be assured again, in our book-lined
Dayroom at the top story of the mind,
That easefulness unbalanced by unease
On the diurnal scale will be redressed
By night, that anesthesiologist,
In the damp draperies of his dark gown
Whence our white throats will finally pronounce
The native woodnotes of our fatal song.
It is not audible. It is not long.

Notes

It's pretty presumptuous for a writer to annotate his own work, but I'm told that the allusions in some of these poems require a clue. Hence:

"An American in Evans Country." Kingsley Amis and, latterly, Robert Conquest have been having fun with a series of poems about a rat with women called Dai Evans, who operates in a section of Wales his creators denominate Evans Country. In this poem, I was spoofing the rather infantile and gleeful sexual rapacity displayed by the Evans sequence.

"The New York Woman" was the headline and protagonist of a series of ads for the Chemical Corn Exchange (as it then was) Bank. Their lady was impossibly svelte; mine is, I hope, more lifelike.

"Pursuit of Honor" contains, as you'd suspected, a good deal of Tarot-pack and Grail-legend symbolism, though it is not arranged in any precisely parallel or sequential way. The children at the Thalia are watching a re-run of *Grand Illusion*.

"Excuse for an Italian Sonnet" expresses a middle-aged writer's dismay at being obscured and superseded by young writers who condemn his methods and his values.

"J. J.'s Levée." Under another alias, J. J. is also the inspiration for an important character in a series of celebrated Irish-

American novels. ". . . and later die" is an adaptation of a line from W. C. Fields. "The Order of the W. C. with Chain" was an ironic and imaginary decoration invented, I believe, by the R.A.F. in World War II.